Icy Magic

Rosella the Rockfish Fairy

BY
AANYA GARG

Pharos Books

Next book
in Icy Magic series

Molly the Manatee Fairy

ISBN: 978-93-5546-496-5
ISBN: 978-93-5546-429-3
eISBN: 978-93-5546-430-9

Publisher: Pharos Books (P) Ltd.
Plot No.-63, Main Mother Dairy Road
Pandav Nagar, East Delhi-110092 (India)
Phone: 011 40395855
WhatsApp: +91 9319228272
E-mail: bookspharos@gmail.com
Website: www.pharosbooks.in
Edition: 2025

Printed By: Manipal Technologies Limited,Manipal

Icy Magic: Rosella the Rockfish Fairy
Aanya Garg

Books in Icy Magic Series

Ocean Fairies

Oceana the Ocean fairy

Anna the Anglerfish fairy

Sophia the Stonefish fairy

Olivia the Octopus fairy

Catlyn the Clownfish fairy

Rosella the Rockfish fairy

Molly the Manatee fairy

Dedicated to

My Teachers

I appreciate your kindness, patience, and all the hardwork you put to make learning fun and exciting for me. You helped me become the person I am today. I owe you my lifelong respect.

CONTENTS

Each of the seven ocean fairies has a magical shell to keep the oceans in order. But Fireblast, a squawker, had stolen all the shells to create chaos in the oceans. The ocean fairies' powers are limited in the human world, that is why they took the help of two girls, Alice and Christy, to help them recover the shells. By placing their hands on a fairy when needed, the fairy's power increases. Thus far, only five shells have been found out of seven.

CHAPTER 1

"Come on! Let's take a stroll in these beautiful gardens." All the kids from the Coral Blue Adventures, a summer camp, had gone for a tour at the gardens by the Coral Beach. Alice

pointed out, "Look, one of the rarest flowers in the world - Middlemist's Red! Let's smell it." It smelled wonderful. Christy also took a sniff and agreed, "You are right!"

Then suddenly something sparkling caught Alice and Christy's eye. The glow seemed to be coming from a few flowers ahead.

The girls got goosebumps for by then, they had learned that whenever they spotted something sparkling or glowing, it would be time for some magical adventure. They strode towards the flower.

There they saw Rosella the Rockfish fairy sitting on the flower. Rosella waved to the girls. “Hi!” Christy and Alice responded.

CHAPTER 2

Rosella introduced herself, "I am Rosella, the Rockfish Fairy. Without my garnet shell, the coral reefs will get destroyed. Sea animals like lobsters, clams, sea turtles and other fishes who take shelter in the corals will have no home and food. Will you help me find my garnet shell?"

"Yes, of course!" the girls replied.

"We don't want sea animals to die out of hunger," said Alice sadly.

"We've got to find the shell," said Christy in a determined voice.

"But where should we start looking?" Alice asked.

Rosella said, “I can feel the presence of my shell. Look at my wrist band– it’s flashing a faint green light. This means the shell has to be somewhere nearby. I am sure Fireblast is somewhere on the ocean trying to create chaos. I will need your help when we find him. Can you come with me?”

“Oh, yes!” Alice and Christy replied.

Rosella flicked her wand, shrinking the girls to the size of a fairy. Turquoise wings grew from their back. They zoomed away, hovering above Coral Beach, taking in its full ariel view. “Look there! Fireblast! He’s sailing in the boat!” said Alice.

"Oh! I can see the coral reefs turning white. We need to stop him," said Rosella urgently.

"But how? I am sure he wouldn't fall again

for our fake shell swapping trick," said Alice. "Definitely not! He has certainly learned from his past experiences. He's getting smarter," Christy added.

"Then what shall we do this time?" Rosella questioned.

CHAPTER 3

An idea popped in Christy's mind. "How about using magic to make a wire net to trap him?"

"Excellent!" cried Rosella. "Help me."

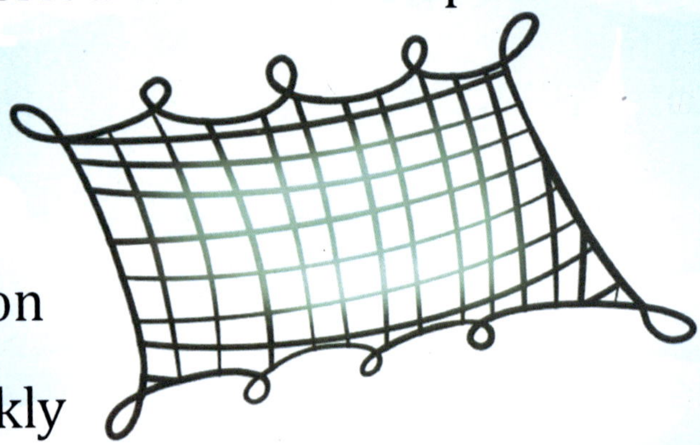

The girls understood and put their hands on her. Rosella quickly swirled her wand and a wire-mesh fishing net appeared. Together they held the net and flew above Fireblast.

At the right time, they dropped it on Fireblast and he was instantly trapped. He tried to wriggle free, but the net just wouldn't let him go.

Fireblast tried to melt the net with heat rays shooting from his eyes, but since the net was made out of steel wires, instead of melting, it just got red hot. Unable to break free, he looked around to find those who had dropped the net on him. He got

a glimpse of the fairy and the two girls hovering above him. They were giggling madly.

He begged to be set free. "Only if you return us our garnet shell!" shouted Christy and Alice.

CHAPTER 4

"Sure, I will!" replied Fireblast. He quickly gave them a garnet shell. It was a fake one. He had learned from his past mistakes. Since he had been tricked by the girls in a previous encounter, he had been carrying two shells with him– the real one and a fake one– in case

of situations like this. Rosella waved her wand to free Fireblast from the net. She was pleased that she got her garnet shell back.

However, Rosella soon found that when she tried to work the magic of her garnet shell, it didn't respond. She realized quickly that they had been tricked by Fireblast. "It's a fake shell!" she cried.

In the meantime, Fireblast zoomed away with the real shell as soon as he was set free.

The girls had to think of another plan quickly. Since, they were flying high in the sky, they could spot him easily. Rosella quickly shot a snowball down at Fireblast, freezing him instantly.

Then, with a flick of her wand, Alice and Christly landed on Fireblast's boat and snatched the shell from his hand.

Since the magic could last only a few minutes,

they quickly flew back to Rosella and handed the shell to her. They smiled at each other and returned to Fairyland.

Rosella returned the shell to the Queen to be kept back in her treasure chest safely. The Queen thanked Alice and Christy for helping Rosella find her shell and invited them to Fairland's quarterly gala lunch scheduled for that day. The girls gleefully accepted the invite.

It was customary for fairies of all departments to meet over the quarterly gala lunch. Alice and

Christy got a chance to meet fairies from across all departments of Fairyland like ocean fairies, earth fairies, road fairies, plant fairies, season fairies etc. They were amazed to see how all these fairies were tasked to make sure everything in the human and fairy world stays in place.

Alice and Christy managed to find six shells but one is still missing. What will be their next adventure? Will they be able to find the last missing shell? Read on in the next book Molly the Manatee Fairy.

Interesting Facts on Corals

- Corals are animals, not plants.
- They come in a wide array of shapes, sizes, and colours. Some resemble deer antlers, and trees while others look like giant fans, brains, and honeycomb.
- They cover 1% of the ocean but are home to almost 25% of known marine species ranging from fish and sea-birds to turtles, sharks, and dolphins.
- The first coral reefs were formed on Earth about 240 million years ago, even before the dinosaurs were alive! Most coral reefs we see today are between 5,000 and 10,000 years old.
- Coral reef systems are naturally colourful because of the algae that live in them.
- White coral is a stressed coral (and that's not fun). Corals turn white because of a process known as coral bleaching. When there are drastic changes in temperature, light and nutrients, corals get stressed and expel the algae living inside them thus losing their colour and the free food given by the algae, therefore turning very

pale! If the situation does not improve quickly, the corals will eventually die from disease or lack of food.

- Unfortunately, 25% of coral reefs are irrevocably damaged in the past 30 years. Destructive fishing practices, coral mining, and climate change are some of the reasons behind their plight.

- They are one of the slowest growing creatures on Earth, with an estimated 1-centimetre growth in height per annum. A coral reef spreading just a few square kilometres would have taken around 1 million years to grow.

- The largest coral reef in the world is the Great Barrier Reef off the coast of Australia. It stretches for over 2400 kilometres. It is so large that it can be seen from space.

Why are corals important to us?

- Half a billion people rely on coral reefs for food.

- **They act as a barrier during** storms and are able to slow down water flow as well as to prevent coastal erosion.

- **Coral reefs clean the water they're in.** You won't find coral reefs living in murky water! Many corals feed on particles found in the ocean which, in turn, leaves the water incredibly clear.

- **They are a huge driver of tourism.** An estimated 70 million people each year visit coral reefs from all over the world. People visit the coral reef sites for recreation activities like diving, snorkelling and swimming.

- **Corals are also used for their medicinal properties.** Today, coral shells are used in bone grafting to provide a base for the body to heal complex fractures. They are also commonly used for physiotherapy and for pain relief in concoctions.

My special thanks to:

My editor, Li Ping, who edited my books with her usual fine eye to details. Her expertise and advice have been invaluable.

My Illustrator, Aru Sharma, who designed my book with patience and panache and rendered beautiful book cover and illustrations.

Released Already!

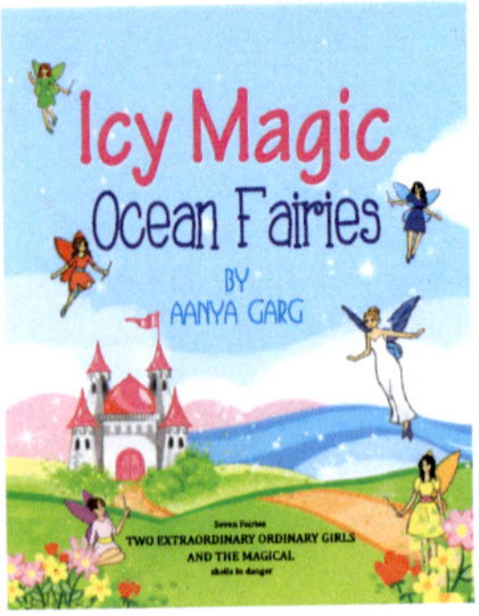

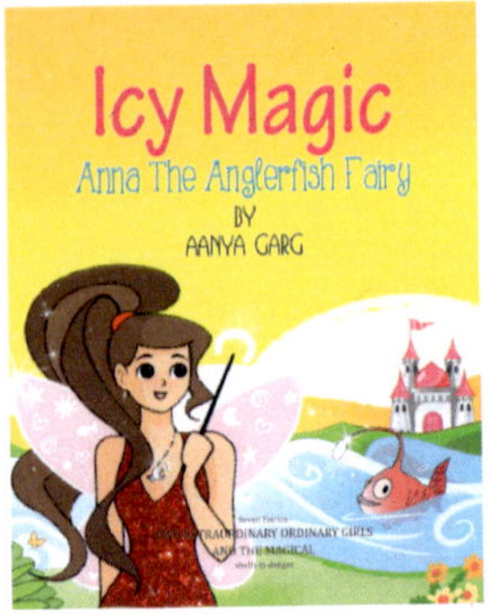

Next Book in Icy Magic Series

Molly the Manatee Fairy